THE AUDITORIUM BUILDING

A BUILDING BOOK FROM THE CHICAGO ARCHITECTURE FOUNDATION

JAY PRIDMORE

WITH PHOTOGRAPHS BY
HEDRICH BLESSING

Pomegranate

SAN FRANCISCO

Published by Pomegranate Communications, Inc.

Box 808022, Petaluma, California 94975

800 227 1428; www.pomegranate.com

Pomegranate Europe Ltd.

Unit 1, Heathcote Business Centre, Hurlbutt Road

Warwick, Warwickshire CV34 6TD U. K.

(44) 09126 430111

Library of Congress Cataloging-in-Publication Data

Pridmore, Jay.

The Auditorium Building : a building book from the Chicago Architecture Foundation/ Jay Pridmore ; with photographs by Hedrich Blessing.

p. cm.

ISBN 0-7649-2496-6 (alk. paper)

1. Chicago Auditorium Building (Chicago, Ill.) 2. Adler and Sullivan. 3. Theaters—Conservation and restoration—Illinois—Chicago. 4. Chicago (Ill.)—Buildings, structures, etc. I. Blessing, Hedrich. II. Chicago Architecture Foundation. III. Title.

NA6835.C48P75 2003

725'.83'0977311—dc21

2003051169

Pomegranate Catalog No. A687

Cover and book design by Shannon Lemme

Printed in Korea

10 09 08 07 06 05 04 03   10 9 8 7 6 5 4 3 2 1

M I S S I O N

The Chicago Architecture Foundation
(CAF) is dedicated to advancing public
interest and education in architecture
and related design. CAF pursues this mission through a comprehensive program of
tours, lectures, exhibitions, special pro-
grams, and youth programs, all designed to enhance the public's awareness
and appreciation of Chicago's important architectural legacy.

Founded in 1966, the Chicago Architecture Foundation has evolved to
become a nationally recognized resource advancing public interest and
education in Chicago's outstanding architecture. Its programs serve more than
350,000 people each year. For more information contact us at the address
below, or visit us on our website:

> Chicago Architecture Foundation
> 224 South Michigan Avenue
> Chicago IL 60604
> 312-922-TOUR (8687)
> www.architecture.org

ACKNOWLEDGMENTS

Documents and photographs connected to Auditorium history now reside in the archive of Roosevelt University, whose librarian, Michael Gabriel, was extremely helpful in the early stages of assembling this book. Thomas Karow, Director of Public Relations, also provided indispensable assistance.

The Chicago Historical Society made their Hedrich Blessing Collection and other photographs available to the Chicago Architecture Foundation. Thanks to President Lonnie Bunch, Director for Collections and Research Russell Lewis, and Rights and Reproductions Coordinator Rob Medina for their generous efforts.

The Richard Nickel Archive, mostly black-and-white photographs by the late architectural preservationist, is housed at the offices of Vinci/Hamp Architects; John Vinci and Ward Miller provided photographs for this book and critical assistance in the historical interpretation of the building. Thanks to the studio of Hedrich Blessing, especially Mike Houlahan and Bob Shimer, for making available new Blessing photographs.

Formerly of Harry Weese and Associates, architect James Torvik, of Torvik Associates, provided important images for this book, as did the architecture office of Gensler, which acquired the Weese firm after Harry Weese's death. Jack Hartray, now of Nagle Hartray Danker Kagen McKay, recounted numerous dramas involved in the restoration of the theater that in the early 1960s many regarded as a lost cause.

Thanks to Professor Joseph Siry for his superb book, *The Chicago Auditorium Building: Adler and Sullivan's Architecture and the City* (University of Chicago Press, 2002), and for his personal assistance in making this much smaller book better than it would have been otherwise.

At the Chicago Architecture Foundation, President and CEO Lynn Osmond, Vanessa Oltmanns, Zurich Esposito, and docent Aileen Mandel deserve special thanks. Edward C. Hirschland of The Landhart Corporation was indispensable. Thanks to Bonita Mall, formerly of the CAF, for her role in establishing the Building Books series.

Auditorium Chronology

1885 The success of Adler and Sullivan's Chicago Grand Opera Theater Festival inspires the Festival's originator, Ferdinand Peck, to plan a permanent opera house, which will become the Auditorium.

1889 Auditorium Building, designed by Adler and Sullivan, is dedicated.

1905 The Chicago Symphony Orchestra, which had used the Auditorium, moves to its own building on Michigan Avenue. The Auditorium faces economic pressure.

1929 Plans to raze the Auditorium in 1931 are curtailed when demolition costs prove higher than the value of the land.

1941 The City of Chicago attempts to foreclose on the owners, whose tax bill remains unpaid. The city becomes the Auditorium's owner.

1946 Roosevelt College negotiates to acquire the Auditorium; it will occupy the building the following year.

1956 Roosevelt University recognizes the centennial of Louis Sullivan's birth with the first of many restoration efforts, beginning with those of architect Crombie Taylor, who starts with the hotel's Banquet Hall, which reopens in 1957 as Ganz Recital Hall.

1960 Roosevelt trustees form the Auditorium Theatre Council, dedicated to restoring and operating the theater as a "civic enterprise." Taylor continues restoration efforts with a survey of Sullivan's stencils, many of which are hidden.

1967 A $2.5 million restoration of the theater, spearheaded by philanthropist Beatrice Spachner and executed by architect Harry Weese, is completed.

1989 *Les Miserables* enjoys enormous success at the Auditorium, signaling new life for the theater.

2001 Booth Hansen and Associates completes substantial restoration work, based on a master plan developed by Booth Hansen. Daniel P. Coffey & Associates directs structural and ornamental restoration of the theater, at a cost of over $10 million.

In a city that has grown large and complex, it is hard to imagine Chicago's excitement the evening of December 9, 1889, when the Auditorium Building was dedicated. A celebrity-studded guest list heard the new building compared to the Parthenon of Athens. Teeming crowds outside, along with the feeling that history was being made, inspired someone to write that the opening of the Auditorium was the biggest thing to happen to the city since the Great Chicago Fire.

The Auditorium Building has changed since that glorious moment. The once-bright facades are faded. Taller, sleeker buildings now overshadow it. The stone exterior looks like an artifact from another age, curious and some-how obsolete. Yet the Auditorium Building still holds a place of high honor in Chicago and architectural history. It was the commission that launched the firm of Adler and Sullivan to the highest rank of American architects. It came to exemplify "organic architecture," the idea that buildings represent an exten-sion of nature. Today, anyone who enters the lovingly restored theater carved into the heart of the Auditorium's interior will experience the breathtaking sensation that Chicagoans felt in 1889.

President Benjamin Harrison, Vice President Levi Morton, and a lineup of other high officeholders spoke at the dedication. While 7,000 ticket holders squeezed in to hear the speakers sing the praises of this new building, an estimated 20,000 to 30,000 people remained outside, crowding the theater's entrance, blocking carriages, and yelling the names of well-known Chicagoans as they made their way inside. The *Chicago Morning News* reported the next

John W. Taylor, immortal photographer of late-nineteenth-century Chicago, captured all the grandeur of the city's largest building, then one of the most talked-about in the United States.

day that "The rills of the population poured into the cross-streets. The smaller streams emptied into the great rivers that surged down-town. . . ."

The Auditorium was America's largest privately owned building and the nation's most capacious theater. It was the tallest building in Chicago, already noted for soaring structures. And it had the finest acoustics in the world. Aside from these notable features, the crowd outside that night marveled at an exterior as imposing as any had ever seen; it resembled a fortress or an Italian palazzo.

Inside, ticket holders viewed the fantastic theater, which was spanned by great arches overhead, almost every inch of them covered with floral orna- ment, bathed in gold leaf and brilliant in the steady golden glow of thousands of electric lights. The great diva Adelina Patti sang, but what was remembered most was the sensation of space. "You could not feel the immensity till you turned from the footlights and looked back under the white and gold-ribbed vault of the body of the auditorium to the balconies, which flattered the eye and then bewildered it," a reporter wrote.

Such adulation was the response that those closely involved with this building had ardently hoped for. Architect Louis Sullivan, his partner Dankmar Adler, developer Ferdinand Peck, and many important investors were convinced that the Auditorium would be more than a promising enterprise; it represented the ambition of a city that was growing in 1889 as no city had ever grown before.

As Chicago grew in size and power, the city also became the center of the nation's architecture. Its central business district, the Loop, became famous for its early skyscrapers. Emerging technologies—including the metal frame and the hydraulic elevator—became associated

Ferdinand Peck was the architects' idealistic client; his conception was to create a theater building joined to a commercial one that could subsidize the artistic mission. The complex and quixotic nature of Peck's objectives—he believed that grand opera could enhance the cause of democracy—was a deep inspiration for Adler and Sullivan and helped them to achieve something that architecture had rarely achieved before.

Courtesy Roosevelt University

In 1888, the Auditorium was not yet completed, but it hosted the National Republican Convention, which nominated Benjamin Harrison. A temporary roof was constructed for the occasion. Citizens were accustomed to construction sites in this period, even if Republicans from more established parts of the country were not. Everyone marveled at the theater, already grand and remarkable for the way it amplified sound.

with Chicago's architects. A distinctly American commercial style of architecture was developed for the city that represented the nation's destiny. The Auditorium affirmed Chicago's leadership in the "modern" architecture, which by the late 1800s represented efforts at home and abroad to infuse new spirit into a profession that depended on the imitation of historical styles. Inside and out, the Auditorium was like nothing ever seen.

The cover of the opening night program (Monday, December 9, 1889) shows the Auditorium surrounded by swirling leaves. The inside revealed that Madame Adelina Patti, the most celebrated soprano in the world, sang "Home, Sweet Home" to the mayor of Chicago, the governor of Illinois, and many other dignitaries. The audience also enjoyed music by Handel and Haydn, and verses by Harriet Monroe, who later founded Poetry magazine. In an essay on the inside back cover of the program, Louis Sullivan himself explained the Auditorium's color scheme. Opening night looked very much like the scene on the facing page.

Chicago Architecture Foundation, courtesy Lucille Knudsen

The theater was noted for many superlatives, one of which was the world's largest lighting plant, which powered 3,500 incandescent bulbs.

For opera, the Auditorium was an acoustical marvel, and in the architectural world a masterpiece of form and color. Lately, Chicagoans have spared no effort to restore the Auditorium Theatre, a splendid echo from the past.

Auditorium Building   Chicago

Hello May.
Mat & I
are sailing
like a
kite. Hang
the best
time
will be.
right prime
for us
outside
when get home
Blanche

With a granite base and upper stories of limestone, as shown in this old postcard, the Auditorium is one of Chicago's best examples of the Richardsonian Romanesque style that architects at the time believed reflected America's simplicity and power.

Escape from Formal Convention

Of the many people involved in making the Auditorium, most notable was Louis Sullivan, who emerged from this project as one of the most influential architects of his time. Sullivan, a native of Boston, came to Chicago in 1873, in the wake of the Chicago Fire. He had studied at MIT but had dropped out because he considered its courses too tied to the formal conventions of the past. He hoped that architecture would take a new turn in Chicago, and he was not deluded; the first architect to hire him, William Le Baron Jenney, is often regarded as the inventor of the modern skyscraper.

After working with Jenney, Sullivan left Chicago to study in France, where he again felt hidebound by history. He next went to Italy, where he marveled at the pure grandeur of its art and architecture, then he returned to Chicago with visions of Michelangelo and the force of the human imagination, more confident than ever that he could make his mark in architecture.

In 1881, engineer Dankmar Adler, with an established practice primarily in the design of theaters, took on Sullivan as draftsman, and two years later made him a partner. In 1886, when work on the Auditorium commission was about to begin, Sullivan was thirty years old and considered too young to design a building that would be the most important in the city. Characteristically, he did nothing to rein in his metaphysical enthusiasms. Shortly after Adler and Sullivan began work on the building, Sullivan read a prose-poem called

Louis Sullivan was the young partner of the Adler and Sullivan firm. He believed that buildings should reflect nature, that architecture was a kind of poetry, and that the function of buildings was to reflect the life that resides in nature. As the ideas of organic architecture became important, the Auditorium testified to his belief that carefully wrought ornament in a building could expand its function to lift the human spirit.

Courtesy Roosevelt University

South Michigan Avenue was the epicenter of Chicago, with the Inter-State Industrial Exposition Hall on the right (the site of today's Art Institute), where Peck had previously commissioned Adler and Sullivan to build an immense theatrical space for the Chicago Grand Opera Festival of 1885. Across the street, the Auditorium Hotel became the primary rampart of a fortress-like wall of buildings inspired by the Italian Renaissance, but the style was regarded as quintessentially American.

In an earlier scheme of Adler and Sullivan's Auditorium, the building had a profile of more delicate mansards and towers, after the Parisian fashion of the time. But Chicago was moving toward a stronger and simpler architecture, of which the Auditorium became a prime example.

Photograph courtesy The Richard
Nickel Committee Archive, Chicago

This photograph reveals the hybrid construction of the Auditorium—a perimeter of granite and limestone, an inner load-bearing wall of brick, and interior supports of metal beams and columns. Sullivan said that the Auditorium "may be considered the last of the old style" of masonry building, although the Richardsonian arches marked the building as "American" in a nation whose architects were still in quest of a characteristically national architecture.

"Inspiration" at a meeting of architects in which he was asked to explain his plans for the Auditorium. "A spontaneous and vital art must come fresh from nature," he waxed, expressing his view that architecture, like nature, had a life all its own. "And so the living present, firm-rooted in the past, grows within its atmosphere, takes on local coloring of identity, fulfills its ordained rhythm of growth, condenses its results, and, waning hour by hour in all that marks its physical, mesmeric presence, fading into the inevitable twilight, it too becomes in turn a stratum of the fertile past."

Some of what Sullivan said touched directly on his concept of organic architecture, the idea that each building, whether a teepee or a moated castle, must be a creative response to its unique conditions, its construction, its use, and the character of its inhabitants. Sullivan was convinced that "organic" meant that buildings served more than people's practical needs; they also served their deepest emotional needs.

The Ideal Client

As an example of the Chicago School's penchant for unadorned office lofts and skyscrapers, the Auditorium Building is atypical. But its imposing mass marks it as a true Chicago building of the period, as does its multipurpose function: a theater, a hotel, and an office block all woven into one integrated design. Another element was the influence of the architect's client. Within the context of organic architecture, the client's ideas and dreams should be central to the design. "It is the client's thought that goes into a building," said Sullivan. "It is the client's thought that leads to the selection of the architect...." Later in his career, Sullivan would battle obdurate clients—and his fortunes would suffer for it. But the client for the Auditorium, Ferdinand Peck, represented the ideal. Peck's concepts for the Auditorium were as complex and far-reaching as Adler and Sullivan's approach to architecture.

Chicago-born and -bred Ferdinand Peck and his brothers inherited large blocks of Loop real estate from their father, a real estate developer, when he died in 1856. For the next fifty years, the brothers exerted a strong influence on the growth of Chicago, taking the long-term view that what was good for Chicago was good for their real estate interests. Thus, when Ferdinand Peck conceived a large civic theater for Chicago, he envisioned not an investment of wild profits and personal gain but a place that would meet the needs of the community at large.

The needs of Chicago in 1885 were obvious. The economy was slumping, accompanied by social discord. The recession in 1883 had hit workers particularly hard, with severe layoffs and draconian wage reductions. It had created fertile ground for socialist politics, and with a dose of anarchism injected into the political mix, significant potential for disruption and even violence grew. Labor went on strike against the builders of the new Board of Trade at LaSalle and Jackson Streets (still the site of the present building). The strike was broken, but bad feelings culminated in the Haymarket Riot on Chicago's Near West Side in 1886. Seven police officers and four civilians were killed in the melee.

Adler and Sullivan's Banquet Hall featured twenty individually carved birch capitals (facing page). The uniqueness of each appeared inspired by essayist John Ruskin's observation that medieval craftsmen often carved motifs of their own choice. Adding to the hand-crafted character of the room were art-glass transoms and paintings of people interacting with nature (above). Roosevelt University later converted the space into Ganz Recital Hall. In 2000, architects Booth Hansen completed a faithful restoration.

KURTZ N.Y.

Photograph courtesy The Richard Nickel Committee Archive, Chicago

Ganz Hall's electroliers were examples of Sullivan's more lavish foliate designs in a building that never lacked for elaboration.

The original electroliers had been lost; the office of Booth Hansen worked with a foundry to design cast-iron reproductions with nothing more than photographs to guide them.

Peck's Auditorium was designed to ameliorate those divisions. He made a formal proposal for the project just four weeks after the Haymarket deaths, in a speech before a meeting of the Commercial Club of Chicago. The topic was "The Late Civil Disorder: Its Causes and Lessons," a talk that concluded with the observation that social stability would be enhanced if Chicago were to build a civic structure to serve all people with entertainment, educational, and political events. Most of the members—grain traders, bankers, railroad men, and retail barons—muttered approval of Peck's suggestions. It took time for Peck and more progressive members of the club to bring this not-so-modest proposal to respectable footing because theaters were notoriously unprofitable enterprises. Slowly, however, the idea for the Auditorium gained support. Perhaps most notably, Peck did not suggest public subsidy for the project; he envisioned something self-supporting and proposed that a hotel connected to the complex would cover the theater's financial losses. Peck sometimes stressed the "direct returns" that would accrue to the Auditorium project, but more often he focused on social improvement and good works.

Peck first put his faith in the theatrical stage in 1885, founding the Chicago Grand Opera Festival, a two-week event to bring European opera to all of Chicago, not just to the elite. The festival was Peck's first collaboration with Adler and Sullivan, who built a temporary theater in the Inter-State Industrial

The Banquet Hall is ready for guests shortly after its completion.

Courtesy Roosevelt University

The polygonal mahogany columns in the tenth-floor dining room followed Sullivan's preference for regular geometry on the ground giving way to profuse botanical and abstract images as the eye is drawn upward.

In the tympanum of the grandly arched dining room, the realistic mural is of a trout fisherman in a Wisconsin stream, appropriate for a dining room whose mural on the opposite end depicts a duck hunter.

Courtesy Roosevelt University

A vintage photograph shows the Auditorium Hotel's second-floor reception room shortly after opening. The luxuries of the hotel included abundant natural light streaming in from the open loggia facing east.

Exposition Building, on Michigan Avenue on the present site of the Art Institute. Already seasoned theater designers, the architects converted a portion of the cavernous exposition hall into an acoustically exceptional performance space. The festival proved a complete success: more than 110,000 attended thirteen separate operas.

As Peck imagined a permanent theater in which all the people of Chicago could seek the diversions of high culture, the elements that created the festival were uppermost in his mind. Investors, mostly members of the business elite, including merchant Marshall Field and grain trader Charles Hutchinson, contributed to the festival and indicated a willingness to be involved in Peck's more ambitious concept. Peck was also sure that Adler and Sullivan could build a new, permanent theater that would be as successful as the earlier, temporary one.

The Auditorium's Technical Genius: Dankmar Adler

According to the precepts of organic architecture, the first rule for the architect is to make a rational and practical building. Its corollary is that elegant form should follow intelligent function, or, in Sullivan's much-quoted dictum, "Form ever follows function." Thus, the Auditorium's objective to be a theater, a large hotel, and an office block in a single building presented a compelling problem. A clear understanding and execution of the building's practical function were required before more lavish elements of style could triumph.

Dankmar Adler's reputation tends to be overshadowed by that of the more extravagant Sullivan, but his engineering genius was clearly responsible for the building's layout, construction, and mechanical systems. His protean

Courtesy Roosevelt University

Dankmar Adler, the business mastermind of the Adler and Sullivan firm, was
a rabbi's son whose interest in theaters and acoustics began when he was a boy
listening to his father speak in various Chicago synagogues. As an engineer,
Adler was unexcelled, and the Auditorium became his masterpiece for its
structural organization and acoustical perfection.

technical knowledge—ranging from the tensile strength of structural iron to the movement of sound through space—was critically important in setting the stage for Sullivan's imaginative architecture to take form.

No one ever doubted Adler's skill, nor his importance to the Auditorium. Adler was "at the height of his powers" when the project began, wrote Louis Sullivan's first important biographer, Hugh Morrison. Frank Lloyd Wright, who began his architectural career on the Auditorium with Adler and Sullivan, later wrote that Adler "commanded confidence of contractor and client alike. His handling of both was masterful." Sullivan acknowledged that without Adler's skill in the practical aspects of architecture, his flights into architectural poetry would have been impossible.

The Auditorium drew on Adler's skills in extraordinary ways. Crucial to the project's success, for example, was his dealing with the sheer weight of the building. Chicago's wet and unstable soil demanded much of architects. For the Auditorium's massive granite and limestone walls, Adler's solution was a unique configuration of isolated piers, each designed to support an exact portion of the building's 110,000-plus tons. The design required detailed empirical knowledge of the settlement issue—Adler said calculations for this aspect alone required five man-years—as each pier would sink gradually into the wet soil as the weight of the building was applied to it. Complicating the problem was the seventeen-story tower—six stories taller than the rest of the structure over a section of its south side. Enlarged piers could be designed to support this additional weight, but because the tower could be completed only after the rest of the building, those piers would settle at different rates. To ensure uniform settlement and to avoid cracks in common

In this sectional view of the building as seen from the north, a complex of hotel and office space is arranged around the 4,000-seat theater. Designing and constructing the Auditorium were triumphs of planning and an engineering tour de force—hotel, offices, and more wrapped around a vast open space largely unimpeded by interior supports.

Inland Architect Press

Although history has judged the Auditorium to be a "modern" building, its foundation
lacked the twentieth-century technology of caissons sunk to bedrock. "Spread footings"
were designed with a precise view to the building's weight and its settlement in Chicago's
notoriously soggy soil. Adler and his technical team made precise calculations, but
because of design changes in the building after the foundation went in, different
sections settled unevenly. Results included curious slopes in the theater's floor.

The metal frame of the space that is now Ganz Hall is suspended at the seventh floor over the main theater space below. Dankmar Adler employed the modern technology of metal supports in conjunction with heavy masonry construction to design one of the nineteenth century's most elaborate multiuse structures.

Beneath the theater's stage (above) were twenty-six hydraulic lifts that could raise and lower sections of scenery with ease and even make the figure of Mephistopheles appear in a cloud of smoke. The system, developed in Vienna, was joined with a 95-foot rigging loft and other mechanical features to make this one of the world's most advanced stages when built. In the 1967 renovation of the theater, the existing system was modified to raise and lower the fire curtain, although the old hydraulics (facing page) have since been replaced.

walls, Adler's ingenious but simple solution was to fill the foundation beneath the tower with concrete and iron blocks before the walls went up, then to remove that material little by little as it was replaced by the weight of the completed tower.

The Auditorium's Invisible Poetry

Adler's skill was fundamental to the invisible infrastructrure, from complicated iron trusses over large volumes of clear-span space to a ventilation system that blew over electric coils for heat in the winter and over crushed ice for air-conditioning in the summer. But Adler's most remarkable expertise was in acoustics. Prior to the Auditorium, his experience in building and renovating many Chicago theaters had made him an acknowledged expert in the field, which was one reason why Peck insisted that the engineer of the Auditorium be none other than Adler.

Adler's theoretical reference in acoustical design was Scottish physicist John Scott Russell, who had studied and written about the transmission of sound in theatrical spaces. Scott Russell's basic premise was that sound traveled congruently with sightlines, and the optimal auditorium design had an upward slope from front to back, essentially eliminating a broad back wall where reverberation could cause problems. He called the ideal configuration an "isacoustic curve," a general principle that could be followed or not followed, depending upon the overall structure and other elements of the architect's program.

In creating optimal acoustical space, Adler learned not only from Scott Russell's theories but also from notable failures of the recent past. First among acoustically mediocre halls was the 1883 Metropolitan Opera House in New York. At the Met, three tiers of boxes on both sides of the theater space necessitated a high ceiling, where sound echoed and blurred, so much so that divas lamented that it was like singing in a barn. In the Auditorium, by contrast, Adler's carefully wrought isacoustic curve was accompanied by the relatively low, arched ceiling that minimized echoes. The low ceiling, naturally, made it impossible to build more than very few spectator boxes, customary precincts of the rich. Happily, Adler's objective of perfect acoustics corresponded nicely with Peck's desire to build a "democratic" theater, not a symbol of social divisions.

A Simple, Strong Exterior

Sullivan used much less exterior decoration than was usual for him, both before and after the triumph of the Auditorium. Sullivan believed that it was perfectly possible to create good architecture with no ornament or very little, which was the approach of many Chicago School architects. But he preferred ornament, Sullivan said, which emphasized the structure of a building and did not hide it. He described the architect as "a poet who uses not words but building materials as his medium of expression."

Critics have suggested that the Auditorium's overall exterior is distinctly plain compared to Sullivan's other work and certainly lacks the poetry of the interior. In looking for a reason, they note that Sullivan's architectural rival in Chicago at the time, John Wellborn Root, had remarked that Sullivan "couldn't build an honest wall without covering it with ornament." Sullivan's plain

The intensely democratic spirit of the Auditorium's theater conception and design demanded perfect sightlines for all, an objective that was largely accomplished.

From above, the effect is one of a luxury and decoration all around, but with all eyes directed toward the stage.

Courtesy Roosevelt University

Although a strictly democratic theater would not have had spectator boxes, the Auditorium's wealthy investors required them. The architects, moreover, were aware that the finery and jewels of the ladies seated at the rails constituted a positive ornamental feature of the theater.

The hotel's main staircase leads from the lobby's massive arch to the reception room above. As nature unfurls its branches, so does Sullivan's ornament, with ever more-elaborate foliate designs in plaster frieze, wrought-iron railings, and bronze-plated newel posts.

exterior for the Auditorium may have been his effort to prove otherwise.

The Auditorium's granite arches and Doric columns represented simplicity and strength at a time when American architects were searching for ways to design their buildings of unprecedented size. Most commercial architecture at the time was an eclectic mixture of Byzantine, Gothic, French, and even East Indian elements—as if perhaps piecing together sections of small buildings. Thus, the integrity and power of Sullivan's design for the Auditorium was seen as strikingly original, though in retrospect it owed much to Henry Hobson Richardson, a Boston architect with highly regarded buildings in Chicago, including the Marshall Field Wholesale Store (1887) at Adams and Wells Streets. The "Richardsonian Romanesque" style was adapted from medieval European churches and palaces, although its rusticated stone and powerful arches were regarded as suitable for a true "American" architecture.

Although it was natural for Sullivan to use the Romanesque style to express the Auditorium's grandiose purpose—its great stone walls and arches celebrated the massiveness of Chicago's largest building—some investors greeted the initial design indifferently and with calls for something more traditional. Peck countered by seeking the counsel of William Ware, a distinguished professor of architecture at MIT. When asked if Adler and Sullivan's design of the Auditorium was close to what he would have designed, Ware answered: "Had I been entrusted with the design of the building, I do not believe I would have reached the same result. But if I had reached such a result, I should consider it the inspiration of my life."

The real triumph of the Auditorium was its interior. Sullivan's massive plaster moldings and other "floral displays" breathed life into the otherwise inert materials of walls and supports. Elaborate wrought-iron railings seemed to unfurl as plants bursting from the soil. Painted murals in the proscenium and on the sidewalls of the theater emphasized the character of natural settings. Wainscoting in the hotel lobby featured the lively graining of Mexican onyx, not the pure white Carrara marble then fashionable.

The Auditorium was undeniably "organic." Plain architectural features were covered and highlighted by leafy botanic decoration. Electric lights created a stunningly rich glow in prolific gold leaf. The arched ceiling not only exploded with ornament, it carried what was regarded as the most perfect acoustics anywhere—as if the distinct arts of music and architecture had become one.

No detail was too small to merit the master's attention; this was the resounding lesson for Frank Lloyd Wright as he assumed the role of Sullivan's chief draftsman during the project. As Wright made drawings of the building's endless foliate decoration, Sullivan exhorted him to "Make it live, man. Make it live," teaching Wright that truly organic architecture involved finding life in every aspect of design.

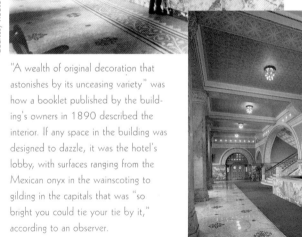

Courtesy Roosevelt University

Photograph © Hedrich Blessing

"A wealth of original decoration that astonishes by its unceasing variety" was how a booklet published by the building's owners in 1890 described the interior. If any space in the building was designed to dazzle, it was the hotel's lobby, with surfaces ranging from the Mexican onyx in the wainscoting to gilding in the capitals that was "so bright you could tie your tie by it," according to an observer.

In the restored hotel lobby, now part of Roosevelt University, the architecture still reflects ethereal effects of stencils and electric lights above.

The splendor of the theater is in its decorative detail, always lavish and often functional. Art-glass transoms (above) separated the entryway from the vestibule. In the great gilded arches of the theater, carbon-filament lightbulbs and filigreed air vents celebrated and did not hide the basic functions of the building.

Photgraph courtesy Harry Weese Associates Archive

In the main vestibule on ground level, the effect is broad and low; its horizontality reveals notes of the Prairie School, which came later. In the 1890 booklet published by the building's management, a writer said that the vestibule resembled "the crypt of some old cathedral of the middle ages." In any case, it was a place where all visitors to Auditorium events congregated and mixed before ascending into the golden space of the theater itself.

Many elements contributed to the Auditorium's acoustical reputation. The curve of the seating, the shape and height of the ceiling, and the progressively widening arches "shaped like a cone or speaking trumpet," as one Chicago magazine explained, were all designed to maximize amplification and minimize echoes. The striking form of this functional element of the Auditorium suggests that Adler and Sullivan made a giant stride toward the Wagnerian ideal of "the complete unification of the arts." As never before, architecture and music became one.

By the early 1900s, the hotel's business suffered because the public preferred more modern facilities, such as private baths, which the building lacked. Talk of tearing down the building and erecting a steel-framed skyscraper ensued.

The theater also ran into trouble. In 1905 the Chicago Symphony, which had been a major tenant, relocated to its own quarters at Orchestra Hall, two blocks north on Michigan Avenue; in 1929, the Chicago Opera Company moved to the Civic Opera House on Wacker Drive. By then, the Auditorium was without a substantial permanent function.

By the 1930s, another effort to raze the Auditorium and build something else was repelled only because the demolition cost was greater than the value of its land. Thereafter, it became a USO hospitality center during World War II; bowling alleys were added to the theater. The building was in serious decline during this period; when the war ended, breaches in the roof were left unclosed, allowing water to cascade into the theater during storms.

In 1946, the Auditorium was purchased to house the new Roosevelt College. Hotel rooms became classrooms. The main dining room, built on the tenth floor partly to maximize natural light in the space, became a functional, attractive library. The Banquet Hall, with murals, art glass, and hand-carved ornamentation, became Ganz Recital Hall. The building's improving fortunes somewhat reversed Sullivan's "form ever follows function" dictum: a vital new function (a college) followed the organization of the building's plan and structure.

Fortunately, early plans to convert the theater into a gymnasium came to naught. In 1960, volunteers created the Auditorium Theatre Council, whose purpose was to

The Auditorium was judged obsolete after the Civic Opera House was completed in 1929. By the 1930s there were plans to tear the Auditorium Building down, but demolition was canceled after the projected cost was judged to exceed the value of the land. The hotel became a USO haven for servicemen on leave during World War II, and among its more memorable features was a bowling alley on the theater stage, with a floor extended over the orchestra pit and into the parquet for the purpose.

South Michigan Avenue has long been a living showplace of Chicago architecture. To the left of the Auditorium Building is the Auditorium Hotel Annex (1893), now the Congress Hotel, and to the right is the Studebaker Building (1885), now the Fine Arts Building—all with variations on the Romanesque-style arch that marked the architecture of the time.

raise money and restore the then-lackluster theater; arts patron Beatrice Spachner spearheaded a fund-raising drive, and architect Harry Weese undertook an emergency restoration.

"It was Harry's idea to get it open," said Jack Hartray, then a young architect, who shepherded the original $2.5 million project to save the building. Remarkably, the old building had considerable life left in it. The structure was fundamentally sound. Some metal trusses were replaced

The view from Congress Street and Wabash Avenue. Richardsonian arches and heavy rustication rendered the Auditorium timeless in a neighborhood of otherwise transient enterprise, circa 1960.

The observation deck on the seventeen-story tower was naturally a tourist attraction, the highest point in the city of early skyscrapers. When complete, Adler and Sullivan took offices on the top floor—a fine spot for the philosophical Sullivan to reflect on the tall buildings that he would design in the decade to come.

Originally, the tower of the Auditorium Building (shown above) had an observation deck (facing page).

AUDITORIUM HOTEL AND ANNEX, CHICAGO

No. 766. V. O. Hammon Pub. Co., Chicago

The Auditorium dominated its stretch of Chicago's most important boulevard and was a natural subject for postcards from the big city.

The loggia from the hotel's second-floor reception hall was a place for outdoor dining and lingering in fresh air. The spot got Theodore Dreiser to "thinking how pagan and Roman it all was," for its massive architecture and the luxury of a place from which to survey Michigan Avenue and Grant Park below.

Preservationist and photographer Richard Nickel had the sharpest of eyes for architectural distinction under circumstances that were less than stately. Nickel died while photographing and salvaging ornament from the Chicago Stock Exchange during the time that building by Adler and Sullivan was under demolition. He took these street-level views (shown here and on facing page) of the Auditorium, focusing on Romanesque arches, Tuscan columns, and great stone brackets, details derived from the Italian Renaissance but integral to the original American architecture in the 1880s.

and lightened, partly to compensate for the weight of the library's stacks above, a live load that Adler did not anticipate. Other Adler-designed systems were functional—the hydraulics to raise the fire curtain and other stage equipment were adapted and reused with updated mechanics. Ventilation ducts, still serviceable, were adapted for modern use, although without the beds of ice that had air-conditioned the theater.

Underused into the 1970s—it was a venue for rock concerts and other fare—the Auditorium attracted new appreciation as a new architectural preservation movement was then being galvanized by the thoughtless destruction of other Sullivan masterpieces, including the Schiller Theater and the Chicago Stock Exchange. From the 1960s to the 1980s, restoration architects took an active interest in the building; besides Weese, also involved were Crombie Taylor, John Vinci, Daniel Brenner, James Speyer, and later, Laurence Booth and Daniel Coffey. By the late 1980s, producers of major musicals found the theater both splendid and large enough for massive productions that toured the world. Political interest followed, with a $10 million grant from the State of Illinois to conserve and restore a building now regarded as one of Chicago's cultural treasures. The offices of architects Laurence Booth and Daniel Coffey have led these later efforts to return the building to a splendor not seen in 100 years.

The renovation, substantially completed by 2000, proved that good architecture does not grow obsolete and that art and commerce can, as Peck promised, create an alliance strong enough to support something as substantial as a building. The Auditorium truly reflects Louis Sullivan's belief in the spiritual side of architecture and the power of organic architecture.

Photograph by Richard Nickel,
courtesy The Richard Nickel Committee Archive, Chicago

The first serious work to preserve the Auditorium began in the 1950s. Here John Vinci, later one of Chicago's leading restoration architects, uncovers a section of Sullivan's inimitable stencils in the theater as part of the project by architect Crombie Taylor.

As part of the restoration project of Harry Weese and
Associates, completed in 1967, the theater's side murals were
cleaned. Sullivan had these painted to emphasize that architecture
of the Auditorium, like all art, was inspired by nature.